Passionate LIVING

❧ a *devotional* ❧

PRAISES

and

PROMISES

❧ Kenneth Boa ❧

Passionate
LIVING

❧ a *devotional* ❧

PRAISES
and
PROMISES

Authentic

COLORADO SPRINGS · LONDON · HYDERABAD

Authentic Publishing
We welcome your questions and comments.

USA   1820 Jet Stream Drive, Colorado Springs, CO 80921   www.authenticbooks.com
UK   9 Holdom Avenue, Bletchley, Milton Keynes, Bucks, MK1 1QR
       www.authenticmedia.co.uk
India Logos Bhavan, Medchal Road, Jeedimetla Village, Secunderabad 500 055, A.P.

Passionate Living: Praises and Promises
ISBN-13: 978-1-932805-93-2
ISBN-10: 1-932805-93-1

Copyright © 2006 by Kenneth D. Boa

10 09 08 07 / 6 5 4 3 2 1

Published in 2007 by Authentic
Cover design: Paul Lewis
Interior design: Angela Lewis
Editorial team: Megan Kassebaum

Printed in the United States of America

THIS BOOK IS DEDICATED TO MY WIFE, KAREN,
OUR DAUGHTER, HEATHER,
OUR SON-IN-LAW, MATTHEW,
AND OUR GRANDSON, KENNETH.

The Lord bless you and keep you;
The Lord make His face shine upon you
And be gracious to you;
The Lord turn His face toward you
And give you peace.

Numbers 6:24–26

"To worship is to quicken the conscience by the holiness of God, to feed the mind with the truth of God, to purge the imagination by the beauty of God, to open up the heart to the love of God, to devote the will to the purpose of God."

—William Temple

INTRODUCTION
PASSIONATE LIVING
PRAISES

There is no higher calling than to love and worship the infinite and personal God of creation and redemption. A. W. Tozer observed that what comes into our minds when we think about God is the most important thing about us.

Our image of God shapes our spiritual direction and future, and is forged in the times we spend in communion with Him. In complete contrast to the world, God's economy measures greatness not in terms of ability or accomplishments, but in the vitality and integrity of a person's walk with the Lord.

When we take time to meditate on the timeless truths of God's revealed Word, we expand our vision of the living God. In this way we develop a renewed perspective about the things that really matter in this world and in the world to come.

PASSIONATE LIVING
❧ PROMISES ❧

When we contemplate the gracefulness of a flower or the grandeur of a tree, we properly respond with aesthetic admiration. Similarly, we respond to our pets with personal affection, and at times to other people with self-giving love. If nature is worthy of admiration, animals of affection, and human beings of sacrificial love, how then should we respond to the infinite and personal Author of all biological and spiritual life? The biblical answer is clear—God alone is worthy of worship. Blessing and honor and glory and dominion forever belong to the Creator and Redeemer (Revelation 5:13), and every tongue in heaven, on earth, and under the earth, including all who have rebelled against Him, will confess this to be so (Philippians 2:10-11).

Let us rejoice as we prayerfully reflect on the wonderful promises in Scripture about God's principles, presence, provision, protection, plan, and preparation.

YOU ARE MY STRENGTH AND MY SONG.

I will sing to the Lord, for He is highly exalted.
The Lord is my strength and my song;
He has become my salvation.
He is my God, and I will praise Him,
my father's God, and I will exalt Him.
(Exodus 15:1–2)

Lord God,

My heart is filled to overflowing with Your praises, for I have seen Your mighty hand at work as You protect me from my enemies. You lift me up with Your outstretched arm and sit me securely in Your presence, high above problems and circumstances of my everyday life. You are my God, and the hope of my life. Therefore, I will praise and worship You with all my heart.

Amen.

PROMISE

I HAVE CONFIDENCE THAT I WILL RECEIVE WHATEVER I ASK THAT IS ACCORDING TO THE WILL OF JESUS.

This is the confidence I have in the Son of God,
that if I ask anything according to His will, He hears me.
And if I know that He hears me, whatever I ask,
I know that I have the requests that I have asked from Him.
(1 John 5:14–15)

Lord Jesus,

May my prayers be in accordance with Your will, so that I will grow in grace and in intimacy with You. I give thanks for answered prayer, knowing that You care about the things that concern me and that You are pleased when I come to You with my requests.

Amen.

LORD, I PRAISE YOU BECAUSE . . .

YOUR LOVINGKINDNESS ENDURES FOREVER.

I will give thanks to the Lord, for He is good;
His lovingkindness endures forever.
I will give thanks to the Lord for His unfailing love
and His wonderful acts to the children of men,
for He satisfies the thirsty soul
and fills the hungry soul with good things.
(Psalm 107:1, 8–9)

Dear Lord,

I gratefully acknowledge the blessings of Your faithfulness, goodness, and lovingkindness. Your perfect character never changes, and Your love never fails. You have satisfied my thirsty soul, and You have filled my hungry soul with good things. I thank You for Your wonderful acts on behalf of those who look to You.

Amen.

As I delight myself in Your Word, I will bear roots below and fruit above.

*Blessed is the man who does not walk in the counsel of the wicked
or stand in the way of sinners or sit in the seat of scorners.
But his delight is in the law of the Lord, and in His law he meditates
day and night. And he shall be like a tree planted by streams of water,
which yields its fruit in its season and whose leaf does not wither;
and whatever he does will prosper.
(Psalm 1:1–3)*

Lord,

It is a blessed thing to drink deeply from the well of Your Word and to meditate on Your timeless truths and life-giving precepts. I want to turn away from the falsehoods of this world, plant myself in Your living Word, and bear the fruit of righteousness.

Amen.

LORD, I PRAISE YOU BECAUSE . . .

YOU ARE MY GREAT HIGH PRIEST.

Since I have a great high priest
who has passed through the heavens,
Jesus the Son of God,
I will hold firmly to the faith I confess.
For I do not have a high priest
who is unable to sympathize with my weaknesses,
but one who has been tempted in every way,
just as I am, yet without sin.
Therefore, I will approach the throne of grace with confidence,
so that I may receive mercy and find grace to help in time of need.
(Hebrews 4:14–16)

Lord Jesus,

> You are my great high priest who came down from heaven to seek and to save those who were lost. Having completed Your work of redemption on earth, You returned to the right hand of the Father where You intercede for Your people as our high priest. Because You know what it is to suffer and experience temptation, You can sympathize with my weaknesses. I rejoice that I can approach Your throne of grace with confidence that I will receive Your mercy and grace in my times of need.

> Amen.

THE MORE I WALK IN LOVING OBEDIENCE TO JESUS, THE GREATER MY FELLOWSHIP WITH THE FATHER AND THE SON.

He who has Your commandments and obeys them,
he is the one who loves You;
and he who loves You will be loved by Your Father,
and You will love him and manifest Yourself to him.
(John 14:21)

Lord Jesus,

I ask for the grace to respond to Your Word with a heart of obedience that is prompted by love. I desire a growing manifestation of You and the Father in my life, and I wish to walk in responsiveness to all that You desire me to be and to do.

Amen.

LORD, I PRAISE YOU BECAUSE . . .

YOUR POWER IS GREATER THAN ANYTHING I CAN IMAGINE.

*God is able to do immeasurably more
than all that we ask or think,
according to His power that is at work within us.
To Him be glory in the church
and in Christ Jesus throughout all generations,
for ever and ever.
(Ephesians 3:20–21)*

Lord,

I will give thanks for Your greatness, majesty, strength, and dominion. Your power is greater than anything I can imagine, and it is this boundless resurrection power that is at work in the lives of Your people. May I glorify, bless, and honor Your holy name with my lips and with my life.

Amen.

PROMISE

GOD IS THE HELP OF MY COUNTENANCE AND THE RESTORER OF MY SOUL.

Why are you downcast, O my soul?
Why are you disturbed within me?
Hope in God, for I will yet praise Him for the help of His presence.
O my God, my soul is downcast within me;
therefore I will remember You.
Why are you downcast, O my soul?
Why are you disturbed within me?
Hope in God, for I will yet praise Him,
the help of my countenance and my God.
(Psalm 42:5–6, 11)

Lord God,

When I am downcast and disturbed, may I quickly turn to You and hold fast to Your perfect character. May I practice Your presence in all things and at all times, so that I will walk in Your peace and power in trying times. I will praise You for the help of Your presence.

Amen.

LORD, I PRAISE YOU BECAUSE . . .

YOUR FAITHFULNESS IS EVERLASTING.

*I will enter the Lord's gates with thanksgiving
and His courts with praise;
I will give thanks to Him and bless His name.
For the Lord is good and His lovingkindness endures forever;
His faithfulness continues through all generations.
(Psalm 100:4–5)*

Lord God,

I will give thanks to You and bless Your name, because
Your faithfulness is everlasting. When I pause and
remember Your many tender mercies, I am filled with
gratitude. May I delight in Your goodness and in Your
faithfulness, as I choose to revel in Your presence and
promises rather than dwell on the temporary problems
and setbacks of this life.

Amen.

GOD HAS PLANS TO GIVE ME A FUTURE AND A HOPE.

"I know the plans I have for you," declares the Lord,
"plans to prosper you and not to harm you,
plans to give you a future and a hope."
(Jeremiah 29:11)

O Lord,

I give thanks that You are my unchanging source of
meaning and hope, and that I am here for a purpose.
Because of Your great love, and because You are in control
of all things, nothing will defeat Your gracious plans to
give me a future and a hope.

Amen.

YOU ARE GREAT IN COUNSEL AND MIGHTY IN DEED.

Ah, Lord God!
You have made the heavens and the earth
by Your great power and outstretched arm.
Nothing is too difficult for You.
You are the great and mighty God,
whose name is the Lord of hosts.
You are great in counsel and mighty in deed,
and Your eyes are open to all the ways of the sons of men;
You reward everyone according to his ways
and according to the fruit of his deeds.
(Jeremiah 32:17–19)

Lord God,

When I consider the marvels of the created order, the wonders of this world, and the awesome expanse of the heavens, I realize that nothing is too difficult for You. You are the Lord of hosts, and You know and rule all things. You are great in counsel and mighty in deed, and nothing is hidden from Your sight. Therefore I will praise You and magnify Your name.

Amen.

In Christ I have a living hope of an unfading inheritance.

Blessed be the God and Father of my Lord Jesus Christ,
who according to His great mercy has given me new birth
into a living hope through the resurrection
of Jesus Christ from the dead,
and into an inheritance that is incorruptible and undefiled
and unfading, reserved in heaven for me.
(1 Peter 1:3–4)

Father God,

I bless You indeed because of Your great mercy and because of my new birth into a living hope. In Christ, my inheritance will never be corrupted, defiled, or diminished. It is reserved in heaven for me, and I will enjoy the blessings of Your presence in the ages to come.

Amen.

YOUR RIGHT HAND IS FILLED WITH RIGHTEOUSNESS.

Great is the Lord,
and most worthy of praise in the city of our God,
His holy mountain.
As is Your name, O God,
so is Your praise to the ends of the earth;
Your right hand is filled with righteousness.
(Psalm 48:1, 10)

O God,

> You are indeed high and lifted up and Your greatness exceeds anything my limited mind can imagine. Surely You are most worthy of praise and exaltation and worship, because Your name is holy and awesome. Your right hand is filled with every perfection of goodness, righteousness, and truth.

Amen.

THE WORST PAINS I WILL EXPERIENCE IN THIS LIFE ARE AS NOTHING IN COMPARISON TO THE GLORY THAT IS TO COME.

Since I am a child of God, I am an heir of God
and a joint heir with Christ,
if indeed I share in His sufferings in order
that I may also share in His glory.
For I consider that the sufferings of this present time
are not worth comparing with the glory that will be revealed to me.
(Romans 8:17–18)

O Lord,

This brief earthly existence is fraught with hardships and disappointments, but I know that even these will contribute to the glory to come. As a joint heir with Christ, I will receive that which will endure forever and will never fade away.

Amen.

YOU ARE THE BLESSED AND ONLY SOVEREIGN.

God is the blessed and only Sovereign,
the King of kings and Lord of lords,
who alone has immortality
and dwells in unapproachable light,
whom no one has seen or can see.
To Him be honor and eternal dominion.
(1 Timothy 6:15b-16)

Lord God,

> You are blessed above all else, and Your sovereignty is complete and perfect. All things are under Your authority, and You alone traverse eternity past to eternity future. You dwell in such radiance that nothing in the created order can fully behold the splendor of Your boundless glory.

> Amen.

THE LORD IS PREPARING JOYS BEYOND EARTHLY IMAGINATION FOR THOSE WHO LOVE HIM.

Eye has not seen, ear has not heard,
nor have entered the heart of man
the things that God has prepared for those who love Him.
(1 Corinthians 2:9)

Dear God,

I do not possess the mental capacity to begin to imagine what You are preparing to give to Your children. The greatest beauties that I have seen or heard or read about are as nothing in comparison to the eternal ecstasy of being immersed in Your triune glory.

Amen.

LORD, I PRAISE YOU BECAUSE . . .

YOU ARE ETERNALLY GOOD.

I will give thanks to the Lord, for He is good;
His lovingkindness endures forever.
(Psalm 118:1)

Lord,

It is with a heart of gratitude and thanksgiving that
I approach You. All things come from You, and I
acknowledge my utter dependence on You for all that
I have and for my very life. You are the supreme good,
and Your lovingkindness and mercy on behalf of men and
angels are boundless and timeless.

Amen.

MY SECURITY IS IN THE LORD WHO WILL BRING ME SAFELY TO HIS HEAVENLY KINGDOM.

The Lord will deliver me from every evil work
and will bring me safely to His heavenly kingdom.
To Him be glory forever and ever.
(2 Timothy 4:18)

Lord,

My confidence rests entirely on You and not myself. I know that You will deliver me from all evil intentions and devices, and that You will bring me safely in the end to Your heavenly kingdom. There I will behold Your resplendent glory for ever.

Amen.

YOUR THOUGHTS ARE GREATER THAN WHAT I CAN IMAGINE.

"My thoughts are not your thoughts,
neither are your ways My ways," declares the Lord.
"As the heavens are higher than the earth,
so are My ways higher than your ways,
and My thoughts than your thoughts."
(Isaiah 55:8–9)

O Lord,

My finite intellect cannot begin to mine the depths of Your Word and wisdom. Your revelation in the created order and in Scripture is full of wonder and mystery, and it is for me to acknowledge these limits when I am tempted to question Your ways. When I submit my mind to Your revealed Word, I discover things I could never have known or imagined.

Amen.

FAITH IS THE VICTORY THAT OVERCOMES THE WORLD, AND MY FAITH IS IN THE PERSON AND WORK OF THE SON OF GOD.

Everyone who believes that Jesus is the Christ is born of God,
and everyone who loves the Father loves Him who is begotten of Him.
Whatever is born of God overcomes the world,
and this is the victory that has overcome the world—our faith.
Who is he who overcomes the world,
but he who believes that Jesus is the Son of God?
(1 John 5:1, 4–5)

Father,

I have come to believe that Jesus is the Christ, Your only begotten Son. This is the faith that empowers me to overcome the world. In Him I have received the new birth and I have come to love You and Your Son.

Amen.

LORD, I PRAISE YOU BECAUSE . . .

YOUR FAITHFULNESS CONTINUES THROUGH ALL GENERATIONS.

Your word is settled in heaven forever, O Lord.
Your faithfulness continues through all generations;
You established the earth, and it stands.
They continue to this day according to Your ordinances,
for all things serve You.
(Psalm 119:89–91)

Lord,

You are the creator of the heavens and the earth, of
all things visible and invisible. All creatures owe their
existence to You, and Your wisdom is evident in the
elegance and complexity of the earth and the creatures
that inhabit it. Your faithfulness extends through all time,
and all things serve You.

Amen.

When I Abide in Jesus, I Experience the Joy of Answered Prayer.

If I abide in You, and Your words abide in me,
I can ask whatever I wish, and it will be done for me.
As I ask in Your name, I will receive, that my joy may be full.
(John 15:7, 16:24)

Lord Jesus

I know that when I abide in You and let Your words abide in me, the things I desire are also the things that You would be pleased to grant. In these times I can approach You with confidence, knowing that I will receive what I ask in Your name.

Amen.

LORD, I PRAISE YOU BECAUSE . . .

YOUR MERCIES NEVER CEASE.

I call this to mind, and therefore I have hope:
The Lord's mercies never cease,
for His compassions never fail.
They are new every morning;
great is Your faithfulness.
(Lamentations 3:21–23)

Dear Lord,

In spite of the sorrows, disappointments, and setbacks in this life, I know that I can walk in hope because of Your ceaseless mercies. In Your eternal purposes, You redeem the things that appear hopeless in this world. Because Your mercies and compassions never fail, I will declare Your faithfulness and rejoice in hope.

Amen.

THE HOLY SPIRIT HAS BEEN GIVEN TO ME AS A GUARANTEE THAT MY MORTALITY WILL BE SWALLOWED UP BY LIFE.

I know that if my earthly house, or tent, is destroyed,
I have a building from God,
a house not made with hands, eternal in the heavens.
For in this house I groan,
longing to be clothed with my heavenly dwelling,
because when I am clothed, I will not be found naked.
For while I am in this tent, I groan, being burdened,
because I do not want to be unclothed but to be clothed,
so that what is mortal may be swallowed up by life.
Now it is God who has made me for this very purpose
and has given me the Spirit as a guarantee.
(2 Corinthians 5:1–5)

O Lord,

I groan in my mortal corruption, knowing that my earthly body is frail and temporary. I await the day when I will be clothed with an eternal dwelling that will display Your glory and will never be corrupted or diminished.

Amen.

LORD, I PRAISE YOU BECAUSE . . .

YOUR WORK IS SPLENDID AND MAJESTIC.

Great are the works of the Lord;
they are pondered by all who delight in them.
Splendid and majestic is His work,
and His righteousness endures forever.
He has caused His wonderful acts to be remembered;
the Lord is gracious and compassionate.
(Psalm 111:2–4)

Lord God,

Your majestic works are evident to the wise and pondered by those who enjoy them and wonder at them. Your craftsmanship is splendid and exquisite, and Your righteousness prevails against all that would rise up against it. Your acts of grace and compassion are worthy of all praise and remembrance.

Amen.

THE SPIRIT OF GOD WHO RAISED JESUS FROM THE DEAD LIVES IN ME AND WILL RAISE ME FROM THE DEAD.

If Christ is in me, my body is dead because of sin,
yet my spirit is alive because of righteousness.
And if the Spirit of Him who raised Jesus from the dead
is living in me, He who raised Christ from the dead
will also give life to my mortal body through His Spirit,
who lives in me.
(Romans 8:10–11)

Lord,

I give thanks that though my body is mortal, my spirit is alive with the indwelling Holy Spirit. And it is through the power of Your Holy Spirit that I will be raised from the dead so that I will be made complete in my spirit, soul, and body.

Amen.

YOU HAVE DONE GREAT THINGS FOR ME.

*My soul magnifies the Lord
and my spirit rejoices in God my Savior,
for the Mighty One has done great things for me,
and holy is His name.
His mercy is on those who fear Him,
from generation to generation.
(Luke 1:46–47, 49–50)*

Dear God,

My soul magnifies Your great and holy name, and my
spirit rejoices in acknowledging Your salvation. You are
the Mighty One who has accomplished so many great and
glorious things in the lives of Your people, and Your holy
name is to be extolled and feared in all generations of
Your people.

Amen.

PRAISE

As a member of God's flock, I have the gift of eternal life, and no one can snatch me from the Father's grip.

Your sheep hear Your voice, and You know them, and they follow You.
You give them eternal life, and they shall never perish;
no one can snatch them out of Your hand.
The Father, who has given them to You, is greater than all;
no one can snatch them out of the Father's hand.
(John 10:27–29)

Father,

By Your grace, I have heard Your voice and am a member of Your flock. You have given me eternal life, and I will never perish or be separated from You. You hold me in Your hand, and I delight to follow You.

Amen.

LORD, I PRAISE YOU BECAUSE . . .

YOUR LOVINGKINDNESS AND FAITHFULNESS ARE EVER-PRESENT.

*It is good to give thanks to the Lord
and to sing praises to Your name, O Most High,
to declare Your lovingkindness in the morning
and Your faithfulness at night.
(Psalm 92:1–2)*

O Most High,

Your glorious name is honored in heaven and on earth,
and I join in the choruses of praise and thanksgiving as I
reflect on Your lovingkindness each morning and on Your
many acts of faithfulness and tender mercies through the
day. You sustain me and give me hope and joy.

Amen.

GOD IS OUR REFUGE AND FORTRESS, AND WE CAN REST IN HIM.

He who dwells in the shelter of the Most High
will rest in the shadow of the Almighty.
I will say of the Lord, "He is my refuge and my fortress,
my God, in whom I trust."
(Psalm 91:1–2)

Lord God Almighty,

I thank You that You have become my refuge and fortress,
and that I can rest in the shadow of the Almighty. You are
the Most High, the Almighty, the Lord, and my God in
whom I trust. I will not be fearful but confident, knowing
that nothing can separate me from Your love and power.

Amen.

YOUR JUDGMENTS ARE UNSEARCHABLE.

Oh, the depth of the riches
both of the wisdom and knowledge of God!
How unsearchable are His judgments,
and His ways past finding out!
For who has known the mind of the Lord?
Or who has been His counselor?
Or who has first given to Him,
that He should repay him?
For from Him and through Him
and to Him are all things.
To Him be the glory forever! Amen.
(Romans 11:33–36)

Lord God,

> Your wisdom and knowledge are unsearchable and beyond human comprehension. You require no counselor, and You have no needs. Instead, all things come from You and through You and to You, and You are exalted forever. The depth of Your boundless riches are past finding out.

> Amen.

IN CHRIST, I AM DESTINED TO RECEIVE A GLORIFIED RESURRECTION BODY.

*My citizenship is in heaven, from which I also eagerly await a Savior,
the Lord Jesus Christ, who will transform my lowly body
and conform it to His glorious body,
according to the exertion of His ability to
subject all things to Himself.
(Philippians 3:20–21)*

Lord,

I eagerly look forward to the coming of the Lord Jesus
Christ, who will subject all things in the created order to
Himself. In that day, I will receive a resurrected body that
will be glorious and perfect, because it will be conformed
to Jesus' glorious body.

Amen.

LORD, I PRAISE YOU BECAUSE . . .

YOUR WAYS ARE
RIGHTEOUS AND TRUE.

Great and marvelous are Your works, Lord God Almighty!
Righteous and true are Your ways, King of the nations!
Who will not fear You, O Lord, and glorify Your name?
For You alone are holy.
All nations will come and worship before You,
for Your righteous acts have been revealed.
(Revelation 15:3–4)

Lord God Almighty,

I gratefully acknowledge that Your works are great and
marvelous, and that Your ways are righteous and true.
You are the sovereign Lord of all history and the true
King of the nations. Your kingdom alone will prevail, and
all knees will bow and acknowledge Your holy name and
Your righteous acts.

Amen.

THE GOD WHO IS THERE REWARDS THOSE WHO EARNESTLY SEEK HIM.

Without faith it is impossible to please God,
for he who comes to Him must believe that He exists,
and that He is a rewarder of those who earnestly seek Him.
(Hebrews 11:6)

Lord God,

May I please You through a growing faith and confidence in Your goodness, greatness, grace, and glory. Not only do You exist, but You are the source of all that is. I will earnestly seek You, knowing that You always reward those who pursue You.

Amen.

LORD, I PRAISE YOU BECAUSE . . .

YOU ARE A RIGHTEOUS GOD AND A SAVIOR.

You, the Lord, alone have declared
what is to come from the distant past.
There is no God apart from You,
a righteous God and a Savior;
there is none besides You.
You are God, and there is no other.
(Isaiah 45:21–22)

Lord God,

You are the only Savior—holy, pure, altogether lovely,
and glorious. There is none besides You, and no person or
thing other than You is worthy of worship. In the distant
past You revealed that which was to come, and Your
promises are sure and steadfast.

Amen.

GOD FULLY PROVIDES FOR ALL MY NEEDS ACCORDING TO HIS GLORIOUS RICHES IN CHRIST JESUS.

*God will supply all my needs
according to His glorious riches in Christ Jesus.
To my God and Father be glory for ever and ever.
(Philippians 4:19–20)*

Father,

My hope for every form of provision—physical,
emotional, relational, financial—is solely founded on
Your promises and power. You fully know me and all of
my needs, and I look with confidence to Your abundant
provision of every good thing that will lead to life and
godliness.

Amen.

LORD, I PRAISE YOU BECAUSE . . .

YOU ARE THE FATHER OF MERCIES.

Blessed be the God and Father of our Lord Jesus Christ,
the Father of mercies and the God of all comfort.
(2 Corinthians 1:3)

Father of our Lord Jesus Christ,

It gives me great encouragement to know that You are the
Father of mercies and the God of all comfort. Because of
Your good, loving, and unchanging character, I can wholly
trust in Your promises and in the timeless truths of Your
Word.

Amen.

HAVING CONFESSED AND BELIEVED IN THE LORD JESUS, I AM SAVED AND WILL NEVER BE PUT TO SHAME.

If I confess with my mouth the Lord Jesus
and believe in my heart that God raised Him from the dead,
I will be saved.
For it is with my heart that I believe unto righteousness,
and it is with my mouth that I confess unto salvation.
As the Scripture says,
"Whoever trusts in Him will not be put to shame."
(Romans 10:9–11)

Lord Jesus,

I have trusted in You with my heart and confessed You before others with my mouth. Knowing that You are wholly trustworthy, I will never be put to shame, but continue on the way of righteousness and salvation until I stand before You, holy and blameless.

Amen.

LORD, I PRAISE YOU BECAUSE . . .

YOU KNOW ME COMPLETELY.

Lord, You have been our dwelling place throughout all generations.
Before the mountains were born
or You brought forth the earth and the world,
from everlasting to everlasting, You are God.
You turn men back into dust,
and say, "Return, O children of men."
For a thousand years in Your sight
are like yesterday when it passes by or like a watch in the night.
(Psalm 90:1–4)

Lord,

I marvel at the concept of Your eternality—You are the uncaused I AM THAT I AM whose nature is always to exist. From everlasting to everlasting, You always are, inhabiting Your temporal creation, but not limited to it. By contrast, my years on this earth are but a tiny moment. Yet You have given me the hope of everlasting life through the life of Christ that now indwells me.

Amen.

IN CHRIST, I HAVE A SOURCE OF PEACE THAT THE WORLD CANNOT GIVE.

Peace You leave with me; Your peace You give to me.
Not as the world gives, do You give to me.
I will not let my heart be troubled nor let it be fearful.
(John 14:27)

Dear Lord,

I will revel and rejoice in the transcendent peace that You alone can give to me. Because I have hoped and trusted in Jesus, I need never be troubled and fearful. You have given me an inner peace that the world can neither understand nor offer.

Amen.

LORD, I PRAISE YOU BECAUSE . . .

YOUR THOUGHTS ARE PRECIOUS TO ME.

How precious are Your thoughts to me, O God!
How vast is the sum of them!
If I should count them, they would outnumber the grains of sand.
When I awake, I am still with You.
(Psalm 139:17–18)

O God,

Your thoughts are vast and all-encompassing, surpassing all the grains of sand on all the beaches of the world. You know all things and all people, and no one can search out the wonders of Your thoughts. You never leave me, even in my sleep; I am still with You when I awake, and You are with me throughout the course of each day.

Amen.

I CAN BE CONFIDENT THAT GOD WILL ANSWER MY PRAYERS WHEN I TRUST IN HIM.

You have said, "Whatever you ask for in prayer,
believe that you have received it, and it will be yours."
(Mark 11:24)

Lord,

May I walk in Your will and desire the things You desire for me. I will delight myself in You and ask without wavering in doubt and disbelief, trusting in Your boundless resources and in Your willingness to give me what is best.

Amen.

LORD, I PRAISE YOU BECAUSE . . .

YOUR POWER AND UNDERSTANDING ARE BOUNDLESS.

"To whom will you compare Me?
Or who is My equal?" says the Holy One.
Lift your eyes to the heavens and see who has created them,
He who brings out the starry host by number
and calls them each by name.
Because of His great might and the strength of His power,
not one of them is missing.
Do you not know? Have you not heard?
The everlasting God, the Lord,
the Creator of the ends of the earth,
does not grow tired or weary.
No one can fathom His understanding.
(Isaiah 40:25–26, 28)

Everlastng God,

No one can compare with You, the infinite and personal
creator of the heavens and the earth. You spoke the vast
array of stars into being and know them each by name,
though their number is stupendous. You order and
control all things through Your sovereign power, and
nothing escapes Your lordship. You rule all things in Your
universe, and I can trust You to order my life as well.

Amen.

When I approach You by asking, seeking, and knocking, I have Your assurance that You will respond.

When I ask, it will be given to me; when I seek, I will find;
when I knock, the door will be opened to me.
For everyone who asks receives; he who seeks finds;
and to him who knocks, the door will be opened.
(Matthew 7:7–8; Luke 11:9–10)

Lord,

I come to You in full acknowledgement of my desperation
and need for You. I am grateful that You open the door
upon which I knock, and that You reward those who
seek You. In Your grace You give me better than what I
request, because You alone know what I truly need.

Amen.

LORD, I PRAISE YOU BECAUSE . . .

YOUR YEARS WILL HAVE NO END.

My days are like a lengthened shadow,
and I wither away like grass.
But You, O Lord, will endure forever,
and the remembrance of Your name to all generations.
Of old, You laid the foundations of the earth,
and the heavens are the work of Your hands.
They will perish, but You will endure;
they will all wear out like a garment.
Like clothing, You will change them,
and they will be discarded.
But You are the same, and Your years will have no end.
(Psalm 102:11–12, 25–27)

O Lord,

Though all things in this created order are subject to change and decay, You never change, and Your power and years are never diminished. You who laid the foundations of the earth and spoke the heavens into being will also create new heavens and a new earth that will endure.

Amen.

PROMISE

SINCE THE LORD IS THE STRENGTH OF MY LIFE, I NEED FEAR NO ONE.

The Lord is my light and my salvation;
whom shall I fear?
The Lord is the strength of my life;
of whom shall I be afraid?
(Psalm 27:1)

O Lord,

You are my light and my salvation, and it is in You that my real strength resides. Because of Your empowering presence, I will not be fearful or dismayed. When I am anxious, I will turn my burdens over to You and replace earthly fear with divine peace.

Amen.

LORD, I PRAISE YOU BECAUSE . . .

YOUR YEARS WILL HAVE NO END.

O Lord, You have searched me and You know me.
You know when I sit down and when I rise up;
You understand my thoughts from afar.
You scrutinize my path and my lying down
and are acquainted with all my ways.
Before a word is on my tongue,
O Lord, You know it completely.
(Psalm 139:1—4)

O Lord,

You know me down to the very depths of my inner being.
My ways and my paths are never hidden from You, and
You are fully aware of all my thoughts. I cannot hide from
You, but it gives me great comfort to realize that the One
who knows me best is also the One who loves me most.

Amen.

Because I believe in the name of the Son of God, I know that I have eternal life.

God has given me eternal life, and this life is in His Son.
He who has the Son has life;
he who does not have the Son of God does not have life.
Since I believe in the name of the Son of God,
I know that I have eternal life.
(1 John 5:11–13)

Lord God,

I thank You for the boundless and costly gift of eternal life that was purchased by the redemptive work of Your Son. Since I have come to believe in His name, I have Your assurance that I have eternal life in Him. May I live and walk in His life and display it to others.

Amen.

YOUR JUDGMENTS ARE TRUE AND RIGHTEOUS.

Hallelujah! Salvation and glory and power belong to our God,
because His judgments are true and righteous.
(Revelation 19:1–2)

Lord God,

My hope is in Your unchanging character and in the promises that flow out of Your goodness. I rejoice that salvation and glory and power belong to You, for You are the source of every good thing. Your judgments are true and altogether righteous, and Your perfections are lacking in nothing. I praise You for Your goodness.

Amen.

SINCE I AM IN CHRIST, GOD HAS IMPLANTED HIS LIGHT, GLORY, AND POWER WITHIN ME.

God who said, "Let light shine out of darkness"
made His light shine in my heart
to give me the light of the knowledge of the glory of God
in the face of Christ.
But I have this treasure in an earthen vessel
to show that this all-surpassing power is from God and not from me.
(2 Corinthians 4:6–7)

O God,

Although I was formerly darkness, now I am light in the Lord. You have given me the light of the knowledge of Your glory in the face of Your Son, and this treasure becomes most evident when I walk in dependence on Your power and not on my own.

Amen.

LORD, I PRAISE YOU BECAUSE . . .

YOU RULE OVER ALL THE KINGDOMS OF THE NATIONS.

O Lord, the God of our fathers,
are You not the God who is in heaven?
Are You not the ruler over all the kingdoms of the nations?
Power and might are in Your hand,
and no one is able to withstand You.
(2 Chronicles 20:6)

God of all,

You are the ruler over all the kingdoms of the nations. You raise up and depose the kingdoms of this earth, but only Your kingdom is everlasting. Nothing can thwart Your good and perfect purposes, for You alone are the God of heaven. I delight in Your power, in Your sovereign rule, and in Your loving purposes for those whose hearts are fixed on You.

Amen.

THE FATHER HAS IDENTIFIED ME WITH HIS SON, BOTH IN HIS DEATH AND IN HIS RESURRECTED LIFE.

If I have been united with Christ in the likeness of His death,
I will certainly also be united with Him
in the likeness of His resurrection.
(Romans 6:5)

Father,

> Thank You for the unimaginably rich truths that You
> have revealed in Your Word concerning the work of Your
> beloved Son. You have identified me by grace through
> faith into the fullness of His life. Because of this, I know
> that I will forever enjoy His resurrected life.
>
> Amen.

LORD, I PRAISE YOU BECAUSE . . .

YOU ARE THE GOD OF OUR SALVATION.

You answer us with awesome deeds of righteousness,
O God of our salvation,
You who are the hope of all the ends of the earth
and of the farthest seas;
You formed the mountains by Your strength,
having armed Yourself with power;
and You stilled the roaring of the seas,
the roaring of their waves, and the tumult of the peoples.
(Psalm 65:5–7)

God of my salvation,

I rejoice in Your awesome deeds of righteousness. The whole creation from the scale of the smallest to the greatest is filled with the evidences of Your magnificent beauty, glory, and boundless creativity. You have made all things well, and Your power is evident everywhere I look. May I walk in humility and gratitude before You, the God of my salvation.

Amen.

In Christ, I am destined to receive a kingdom that cannot be shaken.

Since I am receiving a kingdom that cannot be shaken,
I will be thankful and so worship God acceptably
with reverence and awe,
for my God is a consuming fire.
(Hebrews 12:28–29)

My God,

I want to worship You acceptably with reverence and awe, for You are a consuming fire of holiness and love. Teach me to be ever more thankful, so that growing gratitude will be my worship as I remember Your radiant promise that I am destined in Christ to receive a kingdom that can never be overthrown or diminished.

Amen.

LORD, I PRAISE YOU BECAUSE . . .

YOU ARE EXALTED ON HIGH.

From the rising of the sun to its setting,
the name of the Lord is to be praised.
The Lord is high above all nations,
His glory above the heavens.
Who is like the Lord our God,
the One who is enthroned on high,
who humbles Himself to behold
the things that are in the heavens and in the earth?
(Psalm 113:3–6)

Lord God,

You are the One who is enthroned on high, and Your
glorious name is to be praised and exalted. Your majesty
and splendor transcend all things, and yet You have
humbled Yourself to behold and to be concerned with
the things that are in the heavens and in the earth. In
light of this, I marvel at the meaning of the incarnation
of Your Son and at the suffering He bore to purchase our
salvation.

Amen.

When we walk in the light of God's presence, we are exalted in His righteousness.

Blessed are those who have learned to acclaim You,
who walk in the light of Your presence, O Lord.
They rejoice in Your name all day long,
and they are exalted in Your righteousness.
(Psalm 89:15–16)

Lord God,

> May I rejoice in Your name throughout the day and order my steps as if I could see You. Let me walk in the light of Your presence and learn to acclaim You in thought, word, and deed. Then I will be exalted in Your righteousness, and my joy will continue to increase.

Amen.

LORD, I PRAISE YOU BECAUSE . . .

YOU RULE OVER ALL YOUR CREATION.

The Lord God of hosts—
He who touches the earth and it melts,
and all who live in it mourn;
He who builds His staircase in the heavens
and founded the expanse over the earth;
He who calls for the waters of the sea
and pours them out over the face of the earth—
the Lord is His name.
(Amos 9:5–6)

Lord God of hosts,

The glories of the heavens and of the earth all point to
You. Your authority and power are evident in the sea
and in the sky, in the sun and moon and the starry hosts
in the vast expanse of space. All these are in Your hands,
and nothing can defeat Your purposes which You planned
from before the foundation of the earth, even from all
eternity.

Amen.

Because I believe in Jesus, I rejoice in the living hope that I will see Him soon.

Though I have not seen Jesus, I love Him;
and though I do not see Him now but believe in Him,
I rejoice with joy inexpressible and full of glory,
for I am receiving the end of my faith, the salvation of my soul.
(1 Peter 1:8–9)

Father,

You have graced me with a love for Jesus even though I have not yet seen Him. I will continue to hope and trust in Him in this life, knowing that in the life to come I will see Him face to face. In this I rejoice as I await the fullness of my salvation in that glorious day.

Amen.

LORD, I PRAISE YOU BECAUSE . . .

YOUR DOMINION ENDURES THROUGH ALL GENERATIONS.

*All Your works will praise you, O Lord,
and Your saints will bless You.
They will speak of the glory of Your kingdom
and talk of Your power,
so that all men may know of Your mighty acts
and the glorious majesty of Your kingdom.
Your kingdom is an everlasting kingdom,
and Your dominion endures through all generations.
(Psalm 145:10–13)*

O Lord,

Though the kingdoms and works of this earth all perish,
Your kingdom and mighty works will endure forever.
I rejoice in Your dominion that endures through all
generations and in the glorious majesty of Your kingdom.
May I speak of Your glory and of Your power, and may I
magnify Your glorious name forever.

Amen.

PRAISE

WHEN I LIVE AND ABIDE IN THE LOVE OF JESUS, I DESIRE TO OBEY HIS COMMAND TO LOVE GOD AND OTHERS.

As the Father has loved You, You also have loved me.
I must abide in Your love.
If I keep Your commandments, I will abide in Your love,
just as You kept Your Father's commandments and abide in His love.
You have told me this so that Your joy may be in me
and that my joy may be full.
(John 15:9–11)

Lord Jesus,

May I revel in Your loving presence and abide in Your love by living in obedience to the things You command me to do. May I practice Your presence in all of my activities and relationships so that Your joy will become ever more full in my life.

Amen.

LORD, I PRAISE YOU BECAUSE . . .

YOU GIVE ALL MEN LIFE AND BREATH.

God, who made the world and everything in it,
since He is Lord of heaven and earth,
does not dwell in temples built by hands.
And He is not served by human hands,
as though He needed anything,
since He Himself gives all men life and breath
and everything else.
(Acts 17:24–25)

Lord God,

You are Lord of the entire cosmos. You made the world
and everything in it, and You sustain Your creatures by
giving them life and breath and providing for their needs.
You have no needs, but You choose to want us and to love
us. May I worship You in Spirit and in truth, glorifying
Your holy name in the beauty of holiness.

Amen.

GOD HAS EQUIPPED ME AND EMPOWERED ME TO WALK IN THE NEW NATURE I HAVE RECEIVED IN CHRIST.

God's divine power has given me all things
that pertain to life and godliness,
through the knowledge of Him who called me by
His own glory and virtue.
Through these He has given me His very great and precious promises,
so that through them I may be a partaker of the divine nature,
having escaped the corruption that is in the world by lust.
(2 Peter 1:3–4)

Lord,

It is through Your power that I have become a partaker of the divine nature, having received the gift of Christ's indwelling life. You have called me to this through Your glory and goodness, and granted me the unbounded riches of Your great and precious promises.

Amen.

LORD, I PRAISE YOU BECAUSE . . .

YOU CREATED ALL THINGS AND SUSTAIN THEM.

Christ is the image of the invisible God,
the firstborn over all creation.
For by Him all things were created that are in heaven and on earth,
visible and invisible,
whether thrones or dominions
or rulers or authorities;
all things were created by Him and for Him.
And He is before all things,
and in Him all things hold together.
(Colossians 1:15–17)

Lord Christ,

You created all things in heaven and on earth. All things
come from You and for You, and You are before all things.
Your dominion extends from the heavens to the earth,
and from the visible to the invisible. All angelic beings
are under Your divine authority, and Your kingdom is
everlasting.

Amen.

THE LORD IS EVER-PRESENT TO STRENGTHEN, HELP, AND PROTECT THOSE WHO CALL UPON HIM.

I will not fear, for You are with me;
I will not be dismayed, for You are my God.
You will strengthen me and help me;
You will uphold me with Your righteous right hand.
For You are the Lord my God,
who takes hold of my right hand and says to me,
"Do not fear; I will help you."
(Isaiah 41:10, 13)

Dear Lord,

It is with gratitude and confidence in Your many mercies that I call upon You in times of peace and times of distress. You have taken hold of my right hand and told me not to fear, for You will help me. Therefore I will not be dismayed or lose hope.

Amen.

YOU ARE GRACIOUS AND COMPASSIONATE.

I will express the memory of Your abundant goodness
and joyfully sing of Your righteousness.
The Lord is gracious and compassionate,
slow to anger, and great in lovingkindness.
The Lord is good to all,
and His tender mercies are over all His works.
(Psalm 145:7–9)

Lord,

I praise You because You are gracious and compassionate. Your patience and lovingkindness are wonderful, and Your goodness extends to all who seek You. I thank You for Your many tender mercies that are so evident in my life. When I reflect upon them, I realize that they extend to many things for which I have not been grateful. I will rejoice in Your righteousness and lift up Your holy name.

Amen.

GOD IS THE EVER-PRESENT AND ALL-SUFFICIENT SAVIOR AND DELIVERER OF ALL WHO TAKE REFUGE IN HIM.

The Lord is my rock and my fortress and my deliverer;
my God is my rock; I will take refuge in Him,
my shield and the horn of my salvation,
my stronghold and my refuge—my Savior,
You save me from violence.
I call on the Lord, who is worthy of praise,
and I am saved from my enemies.
(2 Samuel 22:2–4)

Lord God,

> You alone are my hope and shield and place of refuge. I have entered into Your stronghold and in that quiet place I discover Your presence, peace, and power in spite of the uncertainties and tempests of this earthly life. I will call upon You and give You praise, for You alone are worthy.

> Amen.

YOUR WISDOM AND SOVEREIGNTY ARE BEYOND COMPARISON.

Who has directed the Spirit of the Lord,
or instructed Him as His counselor?
Whom did the Lord consult to enlighten Him,
and who taught Him the path of justice?
Who taught Him knowledge or showed
Him the way of understanding?
Surely the nations are like a drop in a bucket
and are regarded as dust on the scales;
He weighs the islands as though they were fine dust.
Before Him all the nations are as nothing;
they are regarded by Him as less than nothing and worthless.
To whom, then, will I compare God?
Or what likeness will I compare with Him?
(Isaiah 40:13–15, 17–18)

Lord God,

There is no one like You. You are accountable to no higher principle or law, for You alone are the fountainhead of truth, beauty, and goodness. You require no counsel or instruction, for Your wisdom, knowledge, and justice are boundless. All things in creation and all the nations of the earth are as nothing before Your infinite majesty.

Amen.

WHEN I RECEIVED CHRIST, I ENTERED INTO GOD'S ETERNAL FAMILY AS A BELOVED CHILD.

As many as received Christ,
to them He gave the right to become children of God,
to those who believe in His name,
who were born not of blood,
nor of the will of the flesh,
nor of the will of man, but of God.
(John 1:12–13)

Lord Jesus,

I have transferred my trust from myself to You and have received Your free gift of forgiveness and of eternal life. Because of Your gift, I have the assurance that I have become a child of God through the second birth that comes from above.

Amen.

LORD, I PRAISE YOU BECAUSE . . .

YOU CREATED ALL THINGS.

You are worthy, our Lord and God,
to receive glory and honor and power,
for You created all things,
and by Your will they were created and have their being.
(Revelation 4:11)

Lord and God,

It is my pleasure to exalt and lift up Your great and marvelous name, for You alone are worthy to receive glory and honor and power. All things derive their being from You, and You order and sustain the universe. I will rejoice in Your perfections and powers and delight in the boundless wealth of Your goodness and love.

Amen.

THE GOD WHO CALLED US WILL ALSO KEEP US IN HIS LOVING GRIP.

I am confident of this,
that He who began a good work in me
will carry it on to completion until the day of Christ Jesus.
(Philippians 1:6)

O Lord,

I am glad of the assurance in Your Word that You complete what You have begun. Thank You for choosing and calling me and giving me new life in Christ Jesus, and also for Your promise that You will keep me for the day of redemption when I enter into Your glorious presence.

Amen.

YOU KEEP YOUR COVENANT AND MERCY WITH YOUR PEOPLE.

*O Lord, God of Israel, there is no God like You
in heaven above or on earth below;
You keep Your covenant and mercy
with Your servants who walk before You with all their hearts.
(1 Kings 8:23; 2 Chronicles 6:14)*

O Lord,

You are beyond human comprehension, and yet You delight to commune with Your people. You have entered into a covenant relationship with those who know You, and Your mercy and grace extend into every facet of our lives. As Your loving servant, may I walk before You with all my heart and honor Your perfect name.

Amen.

THE LORD JESUS WILL COME AGAIN WITH POWER AND GREAT GLORY TO REIGN OVER ALL THE EARTH.

As the lightning comes from the east and flashes to the west,
so will be the coming of the Son of Man.
The sign of the Son of Man will appear in the sky,
and all the nations of the earth will mourn,
and they will see the Son of Man coming on the clouds of the sky
with power and great glory.
(Matthew 24:27, 30)

Lord Christ,

> My firm confidence and expectant hope is in You
> and in Your glorious promises. I look forward to the
> consummation of history when You come to establish the
> fullness of Your kingdom upon the earth. Your kingdom
> come, Your will be done, on earth as it is in heaven.

Amen.

LORD, I PRAISE YOU BECAUSE . . .

YOU WILL JUDGE THE WORLD IN RIGHTEOUSNESS.

The Lord reigns forever;
He has established His throne for judgment.
He will judge the world in righteousness,
and He will govern the peoples with justice.
The Lord will also be a refuge for the oppressed,
a stronghold in times of trouble.
Those who know Your name will trust in You,
for You, Lord, have never forsaken those who seek You.
(Psalm 9:7–10)

Lord God,

You are my sure refuge and stronghold in times of
trouble. I can fully trust in You and look to You when I
am distressed and cast down. You are the fountainhead of
righteousness, justice, mercy, goodness, and grace, and
You will not forsake those who seek You. Because of Your
wonderful character and ways, I will praise and exalt Your
name forever.

Amen.

THE LIVING AND ALL-POWERFUL LORD OF ALL CREATION INVITES ME TO ENJOY THE RICH PLEASURES OF BEING WITH HIM AND KNOWING HIM.

The Lord said, "Behold, I stand at the door and knock.
If anyone hears My voice and opens the door,
I will come in to him and dine with him, and he with Me.
To him who overcomes,
I will give the right to sit with Me on My throne,
just as I overcame and sat down with My Father on His throne."
(Revelation 3:20–21)

Lord Jesus,

> You have overcome the power of sin and of death, and You invite me to welcome You into my innermost being where I can commune with You. I ask for the grace to be an overcomer through Your indwelling power, so that I will have the right to sit with You on Your throne.

> Amen.

YOU WILL BE ACKNOWLEDGED BY ALL CREATION.

You have sworn by Yourself;
the word has gone out of Your mouth in righteousness
and will not return.
Every knee will bow before You,
and every tongue will acknowledge You.
(Isaiah 45:23)

Lord,

All who are in heaven and on earth and under the earth
will acknowledge that You are the sovereign Lord of
everything that is. Your word is perfect and true, and
altogether righteous. Your promises are as certain as Your
perfect and unchanging character. I will hallow Your name
and walk in gratitude
before You.

Amen.

THE LORD IS UTTERLY DEPENDABLE IN ALL THE CIRCUMSTANCES OF LIFE.

The Lord upholds all who fall and lifts up all who are bowed down.
The eyes of all look to You,
and You give them their food at the proper time.
You open Your hand and satisfy the desire of every living thing.
(Psalm 145:14–16)

O Lord,

I am grateful that I can always look to You with confidence and expectant hope. You know my needs and circumstances, and You continually know and desire what is best for me. I ask for the grace of increasing confidence in Your benevolence and power.

Amen.

LORD, I PRAISE YOU BECAUSE . . .

YOUR HOLINESS IS BEAUTIFUL.

The Lord is great and greatly to be praised;
He is to be feared above all gods.
For all the gods of the nations are idols,
but the Lord made the heavens.
Splendor and majesty are before Him;
strength and joy are in His place.
I will ascribe to the Lord glory and strength.
I will ascribe to the Lord the glory due His name
and worship the Lord in the beauty of holiness.
(1 Chronicles 16:25–29)

Dear Lord,

The beauty of Your holiness is beyond all mortal comprehension. It is evident in Your creation, and in Your Word, and in the person and work of Your Son. I praise Your greatness, Your splendor, Your majesty, Your strength, Your joy, and Your glory. I will acknowledge the glory due Your name and worship You in the beauty of holiness.

Amen.

In Christ, I share in the blessings and benefits of the new covenant.

When You promised to make a new covenant with the house of Israel,
You said, "I will put My law within them and write it on their hearts.
I will be their God, and they will be My people.
No longer will each one teach his neighbor,
or each one his brother, saying,
'Know the Lord,' because they shall all know Me,
from the least of them to the greatest of them.
For I will forgive their iniquity and will remember their sins no more."
(Jeremiah 31:33–34)

Lord,

The beauty and holiness of Your law is beyond human attainment, but because Christ dwells in me, He can live His life through me. May I invite Him to do this each day, so that I will truly know You and walk before You in ways that are pleasing and honoring to You.

Amen.

LORD, I PRAISE YOU BECAUSE . . .

YOU RISE TO SHOW COMPASSION.

The Lord longs to be gracious and rises to show compassion.
For the Lord is a God of justice;
blessed are all those who wait for Him!
(Isaiah 30:18)

Lord God,

You are the absolute and perfect and unchanging source of goodness and justice. Your grace permeates Your words and Your works and Your ways. I will wait upon You, rest in You, trust in You, and commit my ways to You. You richly bless all who call upon Your name in humility and expectation and hope.

Amen.

ALTHOUGH OUR TIME ON THIS EARTH IS BRIEF, WE WILL LIVE FOREVER THROUGH GOD'S ETERNAL WORD OF LIFE IN US.

All men are like grass, and all their glory is like the flower of the field.
The grass withers and the flower fades,
because the breath of the Lord blows on it.
Surely the people are grass.
The grass withers and the flower fades,
but the word of our God stands forever.
(Isaiah 40:6–8)

Eternal God,

> Your living word endures forever while the generations of men come and go like waves on the seashore. Human glory is brief, but divine glory will never fade. May I embrace, learn, love, and obey Your life-giving Word in my life, and may I reproduce Your Word in others.

> Amen.

YOUR WAY IS PERFECT AND PROVEN.

As for God, His way is perfect;
the word of the Lord is proven.
He is a shield for all who take refuge in Him.
For who is God besides the Lord?
And who is the Rock except our God?
(2 Samuel 22:31–32)

Lord God,

> All throughout history, the truth of Your Word and Your
> promises has been proven to those who have trusted in
> them. You have been a shield for all who have taken refuge
> in You. You give hope and purpose and meaning in this
> passing world as You prepare us for a new realm that will
> never fade or pass away. You are my Rock and fortress and
> deliverer throughout the passing storms of life.

> Amen.

BECAUSE OF THE WORK OF THE GOD-MAN, I HAVE BEEN SET FREE FROM THE BONDAGE CAUSED BY THE FEAR OF DEATH.

Since God's children have partaken of flesh and blood,
He too shared in their humanity so that by His death
He might destroy him who holds the power of death, that is,
the devil, and free those who all their lives were held
in slavery by their fear of death.
(Hebrews 2:14–15)

Father,

I thank You that the Lord Jesus has partaken of flesh and blood, so that through His solidarity with the human condition and His glorious victory over the bondage of death, we can be liberated from this slavery and set free to be God's people of meaning, purpose, and hope.

Amen.

LORD, I PRAISE YOU BECAUSE . . .

YOU UPHOLD ALL THINGS BY YOUR POWERFUL WORD.

The Son is the radiance of God's glory
and the exact representation of His being,
upholding all things by His powerful word.
After He cleansed our sins,
He sat down at the right hand of the Majesty on high,
having become as much superior to angels
as the name He has inherited is more excellent than theirs.
(Hebrews 1:3–4)

Lord Jesus,

You radiate God's glory as the exact representation of His
being. To see You is to see the Father, and to hear Your
words is to listen to the voice of the Father. You who
uphold all things by the word of Your power came down
from heaven to cleanse us of our sins. You are seated
at the right hand of the Majesty on high, and You are
worshiped with the Father and with the Holy Spirit.

Amen.

WHENEVER GOD DISCIPLINES ME, IT IS FOR MY ULTIMATE GOOD.

Our fathers disciplined us for a little while as they thought best,
but God disciplines us for our good, that we may share in His holiness.
No discipline seems pleasant at the time, but painful;
later on, however, it produces the peaceable fruit of righteousness
for those who have been trained by it.
(Hebrews 12:10–11)

Lord,

None of us enjoys the painful school of discipline, but
my confidence is in Your good intention to work this
experiential teaching for my good so that I will grow in
Christlike character. This brief period of earthly discipline
will bring forth the eternal fruit of righteousness.

Amen.

LORD, I PRAISE YOU BECAUSE . . .

YOU HUMBLE AND YOU EXALT.

The Lord brings death and makes alive;
He brings down to the grave and raises up.
The Lord sends poverty and wealth;
He humbles and He exalts.
He raises the poor from the dust
and lifts the needy from the ash heap,
to seat them with princes
and make them inherit a throne of honor.
For the foundations of the earth are the Lord's,
and He has set the world upon them.
(1 Samuel 2:6–8)

Lord,

You established the foundations of the earth, and You have determined our appointed times and the boundaries of our habitations. Our lives are in Your hand, and it is in Your sovereign counsel to raise up or depose, to exalt or humble, to give wealth or poverty. You alone know what is best for Your people, and You alone have the power to bring it about.

Amen.

BECAUSE I HAVE TRUSTED IN JESUS, I HAVE ETERNAL LIFE AND WILL NOT BE CONDEMNED.

Whoever hears the word of Jesus and believes Him who sent Him
has eternal life and will not come into judgment,
but has passed over from death to life.
(John 5:24)

———————————————————————

Lord Jesus,

> I have heard Your life-giving word and entrust myself
> wholly to You. Thank You for the gift of Your eternal life
> that dwells in me and for the realization that I will not
> face a judgment of condemnation, since my sins have been
> forgiven and I am a child of the new creation.

Amen.

YOUR WORK IS PERFECT AND JUST.

God is the Rock;
His work is perfect, for all His ways are just.
A God of faithfulness and without injustice,
upright and just is He.
(Deuteronomy 32:4)

Lord God,

You are upright and just in Your complete and everlasting
faithfulness. There is no injustice in You, and You are
completely trustworthy. You alone are the Rock, the
unchanging One who never breaks His promises. Your
work is always perfect, and Your ways are beyond human
comprehension.

Amen.

GOD IS PREPARING A NEW HEAVEN AND A NEW EARTH FOR THOSE WHO ARE HIS OWN.

There will be a new heaven and a new earth,
for the first heaven and the first earth will pass away,
and there will no longer be any sea.
(Revelation 21:1)

Lord God,

You have revealed that this present earth and its works will be burned up, and that You will create new heavens and a new earth that will never pass away. May I order my path in light of this coming new creation so that I will live in holy conduct and godliness.

Amen.

YOU ARE THE HIGH AND LOFTY ONE.

You are the high and lofty One who inhabits eternity,
whose name is holy.
You live in a high and holy place
but also with him who is contrite and lowly in spirit,
to revive the spirit of the lowly
and to revive the heart of the contrite.
(Isaiah 57:15)

Father in the heavenlies,

You inhabit eternity, and Your years have no beginning
or end. You dwell in exalted majesty and in unimaginable
holiness. And yet You have chosen to be close to those
who are contrite and lowly in spirit and to revive their
hearts and spirits as they look to You, hope in You, and
wait upon You.

Amen.

God has sealed and will protect all who have trusted in Christ through His Holy Spirit.

I trusted in Christ when I heard the word of truth,
the gospel of my salvation.
Having believed, I was sealed in Him with the Holy Spirit of promise,
who is a deposit guaranteeing my inheritance
until the redemption of those who are God's possession,
to the praise of His glory.
(Ephesians 1:13–14)

Lord,

By Your grace, I responded to the gospel of truth by trusting in Christ for my salvation. You sealed me in Him with Your Holy Spirit of promise and have assured me of Your protection and preservation until I receive the fullness of my inheritance in the heavenly realms.

Amen.

YOU FULFILL THE DESIRE OF THOSE WHO FEAR YOU.

The Lord is near to all who call upon Him,
to all who call upon Him in truth.
He fulfills the desire of those who fear Him;
He hears their cry and saves them.
The Lord preserves all who love Him,
but all the wicked He will destroy.
(Psalm 145:18–20)

Lord,

I give thanks that You are indeed near to all who call upon You in truth. You satisfy the desire of all who look to You and trust in You and who fear Your holy name. You are the Savior and preserver of all who love You. You hold and protect Your people and keep them from destruction. I will hope in You and rejoice in Your salvation.

Amen.

ALL GOOD GIFTS COME FROM GOD WHO HAS CALLED US TO BE THE CHILDREN OF THE NEW CREATION.

Every good and perfect gift is from above,
coming down from the Father of lights,
with whom there is no variation, or shifting shadow.
Of His own will He brought us forth by the word of truth,
that we might be a kind of firstfruits of His creatures.
(James 1:17–18)

Father of lights,

There is no variation or shifting shadow with You. Your purposes and gifts are always for my good, and You have brought me forth through Your living word of truth to become a new creation in Christ Jesus. May I walk in newness of life by faith in Him.

Amen.

YOU ARE IN AUTHORITY OVER ALL OF HUMAN AFFAIRS.

Blessed be the name of God for ever and ever,
for wisdom and power belong to Him.
He changes the times and the seasons;
He raises up kings and deposes them.
He gives wisdom to the wise
and knowledge to those who have understanding.
He reveals deep and hidden things;
He knows what is in the darkness,
and light dwells with Him.
(Daniel 2:20–22)

Lord God,

All might, power, rule, dominion, and authority is Yours, holy God. I lift up Your great and glorious name and walk in amazement at Your goodness and grace. You rule over the affairs of men and nations, and You are the source of wisdom, knowledge, and understanding. You dwell in inapproachable light, and nothing is hidden from Your omniscient view.

Amen.

ALL WHO TRUST IN JESUS HAVE LIFE IN HIS NAME.

I believe that Jesus is the Christ,
the Son of God,
and by believing, I have life in His name.
(John 20:31)

Lord,

Thank You for the grace You have shown me by drawing me to Jesus and enabling me to trust in Him for the hope of eternal life. I have transferred my trust from the futility of my own works to the perfection of His life in me. He is the Anointed One who came to take away the sin of the world.

Amen.

LORD, I PRAISE YOU BECAUSE . . .

YOU HAVE DONE WONDERFUL THINGS.

O Lord, You are my God;
I will exalt You and praise Your name,
for You have done wonderful things,
things planned long ago in perfect faithfulness.
(Isaiah 25:1)

O Lord,

Even before the foundation of the earth, You chose Your people and called them to dwell with You in the joy and glory of holiness. Your wonders are inexhaustible, and Your councils are inscrutable. Who can grasp the fullness of Your will and Your ways? I will exalt You and praise Your holy name.

Amen.

The Word of the Lord lives and abides forever.

Heaven and earth will pass away,
but the words of the Lord Jesus will never pass away.
(Matthew 24:35; Luke 21:33)

Lord Jesus,

I thank You that in this world of change, loss, and uncertainty, there is something to which I can hold that will never disappoint me or disappear. I want Your Word to abide in me so that I will lay hold of that which is life indeed. Your Word is true and living and lasting.

Amen.

YOU DELIGHT TO SHOW MERCY AND FORGIVENESS.

Who is a God like You, who pardons iniquity
and passes over the transgression of the remnant of His inheritance?
You do not stay angry forever but delight to show mercy.
You will have compassion on Your people;
You will tread their iniquities underfoot
and hurl all their sins into the depths of the sea.
(Micah 7:18–19)

Lord God,

> There is no one like You—glorious in might and
> authority, You also dwell with the lowly and delight to
> bestow mercy upon them. In Your great compassion,
> You overcome our iniquities and completely remove our
> transgressions. I rejoice in Your wonderful compassion,
> because it is the source of my life and hope.

Amen.

FROM ETERNITY TO ETERNITY, I AM IN THE GREAT GRIP OF THE LIVING GOD.

Those God foreknew,
He also predestined to be conformed to the likeness of His Son,
that He might be the firstborn among many brothers.
And those He predestined, He also called;
those He called, He also justified;
those He justified, He also glorified.
(Romans 8:29–30)

Dear Lord,

You have foreknown me, chosen me, called me, and justified me, and You will glorify me in Christ Jesus. Your purpose is nothing less than that I be fully conformed to the image of Your Son. May I live in hope of this great and glorious destiny.

Amen.

YOU REVEAL YOURSELF TO THOSE YOU HAVE CHOSEN.

Jesus rejoiced in the Holy Spirit, and said,
"I praise You, Father, Lord of heaven and earth,
because You have hidden these things from the wise and learned,
and revealed them to little children.
Yes, Father, for this was well-pleasing in Your sight.
All things have been delivered to Me by My Father.
No one knows the Son except the Father,
and no one knows the Father except the Son
and those to whom the Son chooses to reveal Him."
(Matthew 11:25–27; Luke 10:21–22)

Father,

I rejoice with Your Son and Your Holy Spirit in Your perfect wisdom. For You chose to reveal Your truth to those who approach You with the trust and humility of little children. I could never hope to know You unless the Son had chosen to reveal You to me. The Lord Jesus is my life and hope, and I give You thanks and praise that He came down from heaven.

Amen.

PRAISE

GOD WORKS IN US BOTH TO WILL AND TO ACT ACCORDING TO HIS GOOD PURPOSE.

I will work out my salvation with fear and trembling,
for it is God who works in me
to will and to act according to His good purpose.
(Philippians 2:12–13)

Lord,

May I work out that which You have worked into me.
Let me order my steps with fear and trembling, knowing
that apart from You, I can do nothing. Thank You for the
good purpose to which You have called me and will call
me. I want to live out this good purpose in my desires and
practices.

Amen.

LORD, I PRAISE YOU BECAUSE . . .

YOU GAVE YOURSELF FOR OUR SINS.

Our Lord Jesus Christ gave Himself for our sins
to rescue us from the present evil age,
according to the will of our God and Father,
to whom be glory for ever and ever.
(Galatians 1:3–5)

Lord Jesus,

You are my light and my salvation, and I will always hope
and trust in You. For You gave Yourself for my sins to
rescue me from the present evil age and to grant me the
joy of Your presence in the ages to come. All glory is
Yours, both now and forever. You are the Alpha and the
Omega, the First and the Last, the Beginning and the End.

Amen.

GOD USES OUR AFFLICTIONS TO CREATE A LIFE MESSAGE THAT WILL SERVE OTHERS.

God comforts us in all our afflictions,
so that we can comfort those in any affliction
with the comfort we ourselves have received from God.
(2 Corinthians 1:4)

O God,

> You have shown me Your tender and severe mercies to train and discipline me in the way of trust, righteousness, and hope so that I will be empowered to minister to others out of my weakness and dependence upon You. May I welcome Your comfort so that I will in turn be able to comfort others.

Amen.

LORD, I PRAISE YOU BECAUSE . . .

YOU ARE GREAT, AND YOUR NAME IS MIGHTY IN POWER.

There is none like You, O Lord;
You are great, and Your name is mighty in power.
Who should not revere You, O King of the nations?
It is Your rightful due.
For among all the wise men of the nations and in all their kingdoms,
there is no one like You.
(Jeremiah 10:6–7)

King of the nations,

Your great and glorious name is to be lifted up and magnified in all times and places, because it is Your rightful due. The rulers and authorities of this earth come and go, and their kingdoms last but for a moment before they disappear. But You inhabit all ages and are Lord of all that is on the earth and in the heavens. There is no one like You.

Amen.

WHEN I LISTEN TO THE WISDOM FROM ABOVE, I WILL WALK SECURELY.

The waywardness of the simple will kill them,
and the complacency of fools will destroy them;
but whoever listens to wisdom will live securely
and be at ease from the fear of evil.
(Proverbs 1:32–33)

O Lord,

Keep me from being wayward and complacent. Guard my paths and give me a growing desire to listen carefully to Your wisdom and to walk in obedience to it. When I seek You first, I will live securely and be at ease from the fear of evil.

Amen.

LORD, I PRAISE YOU BECAUSE . . .

YOU HAVE VISITED AND REDEEMED YOUR PEOPLE.

Blessed be the Lord, the God of Israel,
because He has visited us and has redeemed His people.
He has raised up a horn of salvation for us
in the house of His servant David
(as He spoke by the mouth of His holy prophets of long ago),
salvation from our enemies and from the hand of all who hate us—
to show mercy to our fathers and to remember His holy covenant,
the oath He swore to our father Abraham,
to rescue us from the hand of our enemies,
and to enable us to serve Him without fear
in holiness and righteousness before Him all our days.
(Luke 1:68–75)

———————————————————

Lord God,

It is my honor and joy to serve You without fear in
holiness and righteousness before You all my days. You are
the author of our salvation and the keeper of the covenant
promises You have made through Your servants the
prophets. You have redeemed Your people through the
blood of the new covenant that was shed for us. Therefore
I will bless and glorify Your great name forever.

Amen.

GOD IS ALWAYS GOOD TO THOSE WHO SEEK HIM AND HOPE IN HIM.

"The Lord is my portion," says my soul,
"therefore I will wait for Him."
The Lord is good to those who wait for Him,
to the soul who seeks Him.
It is good to hope silently for the salvation of the Lord.
(Lamentations 3:24–26)

Lord,

I will wait for You, seek You, rest in You, hope in You, trust in You, and abide in You as I anticipate the fullness of Your salvation. You have given me a real and living hope during my sojourn in this life, and I know that You will be my portion forever.

Amen.

YOU EMPOWER THOSE WHO HAVE TRUSTED IN YOU.

God's power toward us who believe
is according to the working of His mighty strength,
which He exerted in Christ when He raised Him from the dead
and seated Him at His right hand in the heavenly realms,
far above all rule and authority, power and dominion,
and every title that can be given,
not only in the present age but also in the one to come.
(Ephesians 1:19–21)

Dear God,

You exerted Your mighty strength when You raised Christ
Jesus from the dead and seated Him at Your right hand
in the heavenly places. You exalted Him far above all rule
and authority and above all earthly and heavenly powers to
a glorious dominion that will never end. I praise You that
it is this same power that is working in my life because
of my identification with Jesus in His death, burial,
resurrection, and ascension.

Amen.

GOD IS THE SOURCE OF ALL PLEASURE AND JOY, AND HE OFFERS THESE TO ALL WHO SEEK HIM.

I have set the Lord always before me;
because He is at my right hand, I will not be shaken.
Therefore my heart is glad, and my glory rejoices;
my body also will rest in hope.
You will make known to me the path of life;
in Your presence is fullness of joy;
in Your right hand are pleasures forever.
(Psalm 16:8–9, 11)

Dear Lord,

You are indeed at my right hand, and it is from Your right hand that I receive the boundless abundance of Your joy and fullness. I will rest in hope and rejoice in the glory that You have set before me. Keep me on the path of life so that I will dwell in Your presence forever.

Amen.

LORD, I PRAISE YOU BECAUSE . . .

YOU ARE THE FIRST AND THE LAST.

The Lord Jesus is the First and the Last,
and the Living One;
He was dead, and behold He is alive forevermore
and holds the keys of death and of Hades.
(Revelation 1:17–18)

Lord Jesus,

You are the First and the Last, the Living One who has
defeated death and holds the keys of death and of life.
Your death brought about the death of death, and Your
resurrection is the basis for our resurrection life. You have
redeemed Your people—body, soul, and spirit—and they
will be coheirs with You in the heavenly places in the ages
to come.

Amen.

THOSE WHO HUNGER AND THIRST FOR RIGHTEOUSNESS WILL FIND SATISFACTION IN JESUS.

*Blessed are those who hunger and thirst for righteousness,
for they shall be satisfied.
(Matthew 5:6)*

Lord Jesus,

This world with its constant appeals to vanity,
comparison, and earthly wealth is too much with me.
Give me the grace to hunger and thirst for the things
You declare to be important. May I long for Your
righteousness and realize that I possess all things in Christ.

Amen.

LORD, I PRAISE YOU BECAUSE . . .

YOU HAVE SHOWN YOUR GREATNESS AND YOUR MIGHTY DEEDS.

O Lord God, You have shown Your servants
Your greatness and Your strong hand,
for what god is there in heaven or on earth
who can do the works and mighty deeds You do?
(Deuteronomy 3:24)

O Lord God,

You are utterly unique, magnificent, incomprehensible, transcendent, majestic, holy, glorious, righteous, perfect, and powerful. You dwell in the beauty of holiness and in the splendor of majesty, and nothing in all creation is like You, for You alone created all things for Your glory and good pleasure.

Amen.

BECAUSE I HAVE BEEN PURCHASED BY THE BLOOD OF CHRIST HIMSELF, I KNOW THAT GOD IS ALWAYS FOR ME.

If God is for me, who can be against me?
He who did not spare His own Son,
but delivered Him up for us all,
how will He not, also with Him, freely give us all things?
(Romans 8:31–32)

Father,

In Your love and mercy, You sent forth Your Son so that we would have life in His name. I thank You that nothing can prevail against me and that You will freely give me all things in Christ. May I live and walk in this great truth today.

Amen.

YOU PURCHASED US WITH YOUR BLOOD.

You are worthy to take the scroll and to open its seals,
because You were slain,
and with Your blood You purchased men for God
from every tribe and language and people and nation.
You have made them to be a kingdom and priests
to serve our God, and they will reign on the earth.
(Revelation 5:9–10)

Lord Jesus,

I exalt You and praise Your holy name for purchasing men
for God from every tribe and language and people and
nation with Your blood. It was Your good pleasure to call
them to be a kingdom and priests to serve the living God
You are worthy of all honor and praise, and it is my joy
and delight to call to mind Your perfections and goodness.

Amen.

THE LORD WILL REWARD ALL WHO HAVE LONGED FOR HIS APPEARING WITH THE CROWN OF RIGHTEOUSNESS.

I will fight the good fight, finish the race, and keep the faith,
so that there will be laid up for me the crown of righteousness,
which the Lord, the righteous Judge, will award to me on that day;
and not only to me, but also to all who have longed for His appearing.
(2 Timothy 4:7–8)

Lord,

I know that I am called to fight the good fight and to finish the race You have set before me. May I be faithful and obedient to Your heavenly calling, and may I long more and more for Your glorious appearing as I anticipate seeing You face to face.

Amen.

LORD, I PRAISE YOU BECAUSE . . .

YOUR KINGDOM
WILL ENDURE FOREVER.

Jesus will be great and will be called the Son of the Most High.
The Lord God will give Him the throne of His father David,
and He will reign over the house of Jacob forever,
and His kingdom will never end.
(Luke 1:32–33)

Lord Jesus,

> You are the Messiah, the anointed One, the fulfillment
> of the promises made by Your prophets in the law, the
> prophets, and the writings. All Scripture speaks of You
> and points to Your work as prophet, priest, and king. You
> will inherit the throne of David and reign over the earth
> in righteousness, justice,
> and truth.

Amen.

JESUS IS THE DOORWAY FOR THE SHEEP OF GOD'S PASTURE, AND IT IS HIS GOOD PLEASURE THAT THOSE WHO ARE CALLED BY HIM WILL ENJOY HIS ABUNDANT LIFE.

You are the door; whoever enters through You
will be saved and will come in and go out and find pasture.
The thief comes only to steal and kill and destroy;
You have come that we may have life and have it abundantly.
(John 10:9–10)

Lord Jesus,

It encourages and comforts me to know that You are the Good Shepherd of my soul and that I can enjoy the abundant pastures into which You guide me. You protect me from my adversaries and deliver me from the snares of death and destruction. You lead me in the way of everlasting life.

Amen.

YOU GAVE YOURSELF TO REDEEM US FROM ALL INIQUITY.

We are looking for the blessed hope and the glorious appearing
of our great God and Savior, Christ Jesus,
who gave Himself for us to redeem us from all iniquity
and to purify for Himself a people for His own possession,
zealous for good works.
(Titus 2:13–14)

Lord Jesus,

> You are our great God and Savior, and I wait with
> expectant and blessed hope for Your glorious appearing.
> In Your love and obedience to the will of the Father, You
> gave Yourself for us to redeem us from all iniquity. I praise
> You that You have called me to be part of a people for
> Your own possession, zealous for good works.

> Amen.

PROMISE

GOD HIMSELF WILL PERFECT, CONFIRM, STRENGTHEN, AND ESTABLISH ME IN HIS HEAVENLY KINGDOM.

The God of all grace,
who called me to His eternal glory in Christ,
after I have suffered a little while,
will Himself perfect, confirm, strengthen, and establish me.
(1 Peter 5:10)

God of all grace,

You transmute my very brief suffering on this earth into eternal glory through Your boundless grace and goodness. I will rest in the living hope of the inheritance that You are preparing for those who love You and have come to know You through Your glorious Son.

Amen.

LORD, I PRAISE YOU BECAUSE . . .

YOU ARE WORTHY OF ALL HONOR AND GLORY AND BLESSING.

John looked and heard the voice of many angels
encircling the throne and the living creatures and the elders;
and their number was myriads of myriads,
and thousands of thousands, saying with a loud voice,
"Worthy is the Lamb, who was slain,
to receive power and riches and wisdom
and strength and honor and glory and blessing!"
(Revelation 5:11–12)

Lord Jesus,

You are the Passover Lamb of God who takes away the sins of the world. You humbled Yourself to the point of death on the cross, and You have been exalted to receive power and riches and wisdom and strength and honor and glory and blessing. The whole host of heaven praises You, and it is my delight to join the praises of this glorious throng.

Amen.

THERE IS NO COMPARISON BETWEEN THE AFFLICTIONS OF OUR BRIEF EARTHLY SOJOURN AND THE GLORY OF OUR ETERNAL HEAVENLY EXISTENCE.

I do not lose heart; even though my outward man is perishing,
yet my inner man is being renewed day by day.
For this light affliction which is momentary
is working for me a far more exceeding and eternal weight of glory,
while I do not look at the things which are seen
but at the things which are unseen.
For the things which are seen are temporary,
but the things which are unseen are eternal.
(2 Corinthians 4:16–18)

Heavenly Father,

The pains and uncertainties of my earthly life sometimes tempt me to lose heart. But when I reflect on the contrast between this momentary light adversity and the endless weight of glory, intimacy, beauty, and adventure in the heavenly realms in Your presence, I am strengthened and encouraged.

Amen.

LORD, I PRAISE YOU BECAUSE . . .

YOUR NAME WILL BE GREAT AMONG THE NATIONS.

From the rising to the setting of the sun,
Your name will be great among the nations.
In every place incense and pure offerings will be brought to Your name,
for Your name will be great among the nations.
(Malachi 1:11)

Lord God,

Your name is great and wondrous, and it is to be exalted among the nations. The day will come when You return and Your will is done on earth as it is in heaven. All nations will honor the Lord Jesus, and He will reign on the throne of David. I worship You—Father, Son, and Holy Spirit—and rejoice in Your glory and Your salvation.

Amen.

THE SOVEREIGN LORD OF CREATION RULES OVER ALL THINGS, AND NOTHING CAN THWART HIS EXCELLENT PURPOSES.

The Lord of hosts has sworn,
"Surely, as I have thought, so it will be,
and as I have purposed, so it will stand.
For the Lord of hosts has purposed, and who can annul it?
His hand is stretched out, and who can turn it back?
(Isaiah 14:24, 27)

O Lord,

I revel in the goodness of Your intentions and plans, knowing that You always desire what is best for Your people. You rule over all that is in heaven and on earth and under the earth, and no purpose of Yours can be annulled. When You stretch out Your hand, nothing can turn it back.

Amen.

YOU HAVE BESTOWED YOUR GRACE UPON US.

*God chose me in Christ before the foundation of the world
to be holy and blameless in His sight.
In love He predestined me to be adopted
as His son through Jesus Christ,
according to the good pleasure of His will,
to the praise of the glory of His grace,
which He bestowed upon me in the One He loves.
(Ephesians 1:4–6)*

Father,

I give thanks that in Your great love You chose me even before the foundation of the world to be Your adopted child through Your Son Jesus Christ. This was according to the good pleasure of Your will and to the praise of the glory of Your grace which You bestowed upon me in Him. I rejoice that I have been embraced by Your love.

Amen.

PROMISE

THOSE WHO SERVE AND FOLLOW THE LORD WILL BE HONORED BY HIS PRESENCE.

If anyone serves You, he must follow You;
and where You are, Your servant also will be.
If anyone serves You, the Father will honor him.
(John 12:26)

Lord Jesus,

May I learn to serve You and follow You wherever You lead me to go so that I will abide in You and enjoy Your manifest presence in my life. I am grateful that You honor those who serve You. Teach me what it means to serve You in the daily details of life.

Amen.

LORD, I PRAISE YOU BECAUSE . . .

YOU ARE COMPASSIONATE AND GRACIOUS.

*The Lord, the Lord God,
is compassionate and gracious, slow to anger,
and abounding in lovingkindness and truth,
maintaining love to thousands,
and forgiving iniquity, transgression, and sin.
(Exodus 34:6–7)*

Lord God,

I stand amazed at the beauty of Your attributes: Your perfect compassion, Your boundless grace, Your infinite patience, Your abundant lovingkindness, Your wonderful truth, Your intense love, and Your wonderful forgiveness. Because of who You are, I can walk in faith, hope, and love.

Amen.

AS I TURN FROM DEPENDENCE ON MYSELF TO DEPENDENCE ON CHRIST, I DISCOVER HIS POWER IN MY LIFE.

*Your grace is sufficient for me,
for Your power is made perfect in weakness.
Therefore, I will boast all the more gladly in my weaknesses,
that the power of Christ may rest upon me.
Therefore, I can be content in weaknesses,
in insults, in hardships, in persecutions,
in difficulties, for Christ's sake.
For when I am weak, then I am strong.
(2 Corinthians 12:9–10)*

Lord God,

Teach me to realize that Your grace is always sufficient for me. It is foolish to rely on the weakness of the flesh when I can walk in the power of Christ who lives in me. May I discover His strength by acknowledging my weakness, even in those areas in which I am tempted to think I am competent.

Amen.

LORD, I PRAISE YOU BECAUSE . . .

YOU ARE THE KING ETERNAL, IMMORTAL, INVISIBLE.

To the King eternal, immortal, invisible,
the only God,
be honor and glory for ever and ever.
(1 Timothy 1:17)

O Lord my King,

In Your essence You are incomprehensible and mysterious. You have revealed that You are eternal, immortal, and invisible, and that Your transcendent majesty is boundless. And yet You choose to want us for Yourself and give us the gift of Your indwelling Spirit. To You be honor and glory forever and ever.

Amen.

WHEN I COME CLOSER TO CHRIST, HE TAKES MY BURDENS AND GIVES ME HIS PEACE.

*Lord, You have said, "Come to Me,
all you who labor and are heavy laden, and I will give you rest.
Take My yoke upon you and learn from Me,
for I am gentle and humble in heart,
and you will find rest for your souls.
For My yoke is easy, and My burden is light."
(Matthew 11:28–30)*

Lord,

It is only in You that I can find rest for my soul. When I take Your yoke upon me and learn from You, I discover the ease of Your yoke and the lightness of Your burden. Grant me a growing awareness of Your peace and presence.

Amen.

LORD, I PRAISE YOU BECAUSE . . .

YOU ARE MIGHTY AND AWESOME.

*The Lord my God is God of gods
and Lord of lords, the great God,
mighty and awesome,
who shows no partiality and accepts no bribes.
He executes justice for the fatherless and the widow
and loves the alien, giving him food and clothing.
(Deuteronomy 10:17–18)*

O Lord my God,

You are the mighty and awesome God of gods and Lord of
lords. I praise You that You show no partiality and accept
no bribes, but that You execute justice for those who are
in need. My hope is fixed on Your unchanging character
and on Your gracious promises, and I give thanks for who
You are.

Amen.

Because I have trusted in Jesus, I am assured of His resurrected life.

Jesus said to Martha, "I am the resurrection and the life.
He who believes in Me will live, even though he dies;
and whoever lives and believes in Me will never die."
(John 11:25–26)

Lord Jesus,

I give thanks for Your assurance that I have been delivered from the kingdom of sin and death and have been transferred to the kingdom of Your righteousness and life. Grant me the grace of growing trust in Your person and promises.

Amen.

LORD, I PRAISE YOU BECAUSE . . .

YOU ARE THE AUTHOR OF OUR SALVATION.

A great multitude, which no one could number,
from all nations and tribes and peoples and languages
will stand before the throne and before the Lamb,
clothed with white robes with palm branches in their hands,
and will cry out with a loud voice,
"Salvation belongs to our God, who sits on the throne,
and to the Lamb!"
(Revelation 7:9–10)

Lord God,

Salvation belongs to the triune God—Father, Son, and Holy Spirit. You chose us for Yourself, redeemed us with the blood of Christ, and regenerated us through the power of Your Holy Spirit. You are to be exalted and magnified by the great host of Your creatures because of who You are and what You have done.

Amen.

THE LORD IS MY HELPER AND KEEPER WHO WATCHES OVER MY STEPS AND PRESERVES MY SOUL.

I lift up my eyes to the hills—where does my help come from?
My help comes from the Lord, who made heaven and earth.
He will not allow my foot to slip;
He who watches over me will not slumber.
The Lord is my keeper; the Lord is my shade at my right hand.
The sun will not harm me by day, nor the moon by night.
The Lord will keep me from all evil; He will preserve my soul.
The Lord will watch over my coming and going
from this time forth and forever.
(Psalm 121:1–3, 5–8)

Lord,

I look to You for my help and protection in this uncertain world. You protect me from evil and preserve my soul. When I suffer pain and loss, even then I know that You will use it for my ultimate good by drawing me ever closer to You. My hope is centered on You and on Your ever-present care.

Amen.

LORD, I PRAISE YOU BECAUSE . . .

YOUR RIGHTEOUSNESS AND WONDERS ARE MEASURELESS.

My mouth will tell of Your righteousness
and of Your salvation all day long,
though I know not its measure.
I will come in the strength of the Lord God;
I will proclaim Your righteousness, Yours alone.
Since my youth, O God, You have taught me,
and to this day I declare Your wondrous deeds.
(Psalm 71:15–17)

O God,

I will rejoice and exult in Your righteousness, a
righteousness that is perfect, holy, pure, good, loving,
patient, just, compassionate, and altogether lovely. It
is through Your salvation that I have meaning and hope
in this world, and Your presence is ever with me. It is
Your strength that sustains me, and I will proclaim Your
measureless righteousness and salvation to the glory of
Your name.

Amen.

THE LORD SATISFIES MY SPIRITUAL THIRST BY INVITING ME TO DRINK FREELY FROM THE WATER OF LIFE.

You are the Alpha and the Omega,
the Beginning and the End.
To him who is thirsty,
You will give to drink without cost
from the spring of the water of life.
He who overcomes will inherit all this,
and You will be his God and he will be Your son.
(Revelation 21:6–7)

O Lord,

I rejoice that You are the Alpha and the Omega, the Beginning and the End, and I thank Your for Your invitation to drink without cost from the spring of the water of life. May I live in Your strength and lay hold of Your abundant inheritance.

Amen.

LORD, I PRAISE YOU BECAUSE . . .

YOU LOVE ME AND PROTECT ME.

Who shall separate me from the love of Christ?
Shall tribulation, or distress, or persecution,
or famine, or nakedness, or danger, or sword?
As it is written:"For Your sake we face death all day long;
we are considered as sheep to be slaughtered."
Yet in all these things I am are more than a conqueror
through Him who loved me.
(Romans 8:35–37)

Lord Jesus,

Nothing at all can separate me from Your causeless, measureless, and ceaseless love. No person or force in heaven, on earth, or under the earth can remove me from Your loving grip, for You are Lord of all. In spite of the afflictions, adversities, setbacks, and uncertainties of this earthly life, I am secure in You.

Amen.

BECAUSE I AM NOW ALIVE TO CHRIST, I AM NO LONGER UNDER THE DOMINION OF SIN.

If I died with Christ,
I believe that I will also live with Him,
knowing that Christ, having been raised from the dead,
cannot die again; death no longer has dominion over Him.
For the death that He died, He died to sin once for all;
but the life that He lives, He lives to God.
In the same way, I must consider myself to be dead to sin,
but alive to God in Christ Jesus.
(Romans 6:8–11)

Lord Jesus,

It is a marvel that I have died with You and that I will also live with You in the ages to come. May I experience a growing realization that since I am now alive to God in Christ Jesus, I have died to the dominion of sin in my life.

Amen.

LORD, I PRAISE YOU BECAUSE . . .

YOU ARE WORTHY OF GLORY, MAJESTY, DOMINION, AND AUTHORITY.

To the only God our Savior,
through Jesus Christ our Lord,
be glory, majesty, dominion, and authority,
before all ages and now and forever. Amen.
(Jude 25)

Lord God,

> You are the only God and Savior, and Jesus Christ is the glorious King of kings and Lord of lords who purchased us and liberated us from our bondage to sin and death. All glory, majesty, dominion, and authority is Yours, O Lord, before all ages, now, and forever.

> Amen.

WHATEVER I DO FOR THE SAKE OF JESUS WILL NOT BE IN VAIN, BUT WILL ALWAYS ENDURE.

Thanks be to God,
who gives us the victory through our Lord Jesus Christ.
Therefore I will be steadfast, immovable,
abounding in the work of the Lord,
knowing that my labor in the Lord is not in vain.
(1 Corinthians 15:57–58)

Lord,

I am grateful for the victory that You have won for me through my Lord Jesus Christ. Because my life is now in Him, the things I do for His sake will go on into eternity. My labor is not in vain, but will bear lasting fruit as I walk in the power of Your Spirit.

Amen.

LORD, I PRAISE YOU BECAUSE . . .

YOUR DOMINION IS AN ETERNAL DOMINION.

*The Most High is sovereign over the kingdoms of men and gives them
to whomever He wishes and sets over them the lowliest of men.
I will bless the Most High and praise and honor Him who lives forever.
His dominion is an eternal dominion, and His kingdom
endures from generation to generation.
He regards all the inhabitants of the earth as nothing, and does as He
pleases with the host of heaven and the inhabitants of the earth.
No one can hold back His hand or say to Him:
"What have You done?"
I praise, exalt, and honor the King of heaven,
for all His works are true, and all His ways are just,
and He is able to humble those who walk in pride.
(Daniel 4:17, 34–35, 37)*

God Most High,

> I will bless and honor You, the Most High, who lives
> forever. You rule in the splendor of sovereignty over
> all kingdoms and all creation, and Your dominion is
> everlasting. You do all that You please with the host of
> heaven and the inhabitants of the earth, and all Your
> works are true and Your ways just. Your name is praised
> above all.

Amen.

My life is hidden with Christ in God, and I will appear with Him in glory.

Since I have been raised with Christ,
I should seek the things above,
where Christ is seated at the right hand of God.
I will set my mind on the things above,
not on the things on the earth,
for I died, and my life is now hidden with Christ in God.
When Christ who is my life appears,
then I also will appear with Him in glory.
(Colossians 3:1–4)

Lord Christ,

You are in me, and I am in You. I choose to believe that I am seated at the right hand of the Father with You, even though this is contrary to my feelings and experiences. In this life I walk by faith, but the day is coming when I will appear with You in glory.

Amen.

LORD, I PRAISE YOU BECAUSE . . .

YOU ARE EXALTED AS HEAD OVER ALL.

Yours, O Lord, is the greatness and the power
and the glory and the victory and the majesty,
for everything in heaven and earth is Yours.
Yours, O Lord, is the kingdom,
and You are exalted as head over all.
Both riches and honor come from You,
and You are the ruler of all things.
In Your hand is power and might
to exalt and to give strength to all.
Therefore, my God, I give You thanks
and praise Your glorious name.
All things come from You,
and I can only give You what comes from Your hand.
(1 Chronicles 29:11–14)

O Lord,

You are exalted as head over all things, and it is from Your
hand that every good gift is given. You are awesome in
power and in might, and all greatness, glory, victory, and
majesty is Yours, O Lord. I give You thanks and bless and
praise Your glorious name. All that I am and have comes
from You, and I offer myself to You as a living sacrifice.

Amen.

GOD IS IN CONTROL OF ALL THINGS, AND HE HAS MY BEST INTERESTS AT HEART.

The Lord reigns; He is clothed with majesty;
the Lord is robed in majesty and is armed with strength.
Indeed, the world is firmly established;
it cannot be moved.
Your throne is established from of old;
You are from everlasting.
Your testimonies stand firm;
holiness adorns Your house, O Lord, forever.
(Psalm 93:1–2, 5)

O Lord,

It gives me real comfort to know that Your character never changes and that Your promises stand firm forever. Nothing can thwart Your good plans, and knowing this gives me great assurance in this world of turmoil, change, and uncertainty. My confidence is in Your goodness and majesty.

Amen.

LORD, I PRAISE YOU BECAUSE . . .

YOU WILL TREASURE YOUR SERVANTS FOREVER.

There will no longer be any curse.
The throne of God and of the Lamb will be in the new Jerusalem,
and His servants will serve Him.
They will see His face, and His name will be on their foreheads.
And there will be no night there;
they will not need the light of a lamp or the light of the sun,
for the Lord God will give them light.
And they shall reign for ever and ever.
(Revelation 22:3–5)

Lord God,

I look with great anticipation at the promise of Your heavenly kingdom in which there will be no night, no curse, no death, no sickness, no mourning, and no crying. You will make all things new, and we will behold the light and beauty of Your face. I praise You for the hope of heaven and the glories of the age to come.

Amen.

GOD IS PREPARING A PLACE FOR ME SO THAT I CAN LIVE WITH HIM FOREVER.

In My Father's house are many dwellings;
if it were not so, I would have told you.
I am going there to prepare a place for you.
And if I go and prepare a place for you,
I will come again and receive you to Myself,
that you also may be where I am.
(John 14:2–3)

Lord Jesus,

Your love and care for me is beyond my imagination. I can barely comprehend that You have prepared a special place for me in Your Father's house. As I pause throughout the day, I will dream of the warmth and beauty of my heavenly home and with joy and excitement, I will anticipate the day when I shall meet You there and speak with You face to face.

Amen.

LORD, I PRAISE YOU BECAUSE . . .

YOU HAVE CLOTHED ME WITH THE GARMENTS OF SALVATION.

I will greatly rejoice in the Lord;
my soul will be joyful in my God.
For He has clothed me with garments of salvation
and arrayed me in a robe of righteousness,
as a bridegroom decks himself with ornaments,
and as a bride adorns herself with her jewels.
(Isaiah 61:10)

Lord God,

I bless and exalt Your high, majestic, wonderful, awesome, and holy name. My soul will rejoice in the Lord who has clothed me with the garments of salvation. You have arrayed me in the robe of the righteousness of Christ, and You have blessed me with His indwelling life. I praise You that You will come again and receive me to Yourself, so that where You are, there I will be also.

Amen.

ABOUT THE AUTHOR

Kenneth Boa is engaged in a ministry of relational evangelism and discipleship, teaching, writing, and speaking. He holds a B.S. from Case Institute of Technology, a Th.M. from Dallas Theological Seminary, a Ph.D. from New York University, and a D.Phil. from the University of Oxford in England.

He is the President of Reflections Ministries, an organization that seeks to encourage, teach, and equip people to know Christ, follow Him, become progressively conformed to His image, and reproduce His life in others.

Dr. Boa writes a free monthly teaching letter called *Reflections*. If you would like to be on the mailing list, visit www.KenBoa.org or call 800-DRAW-NEAR (800-372-9632).

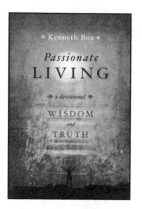

PASSIONATE LIVING
WISDOM AND TRUTH

These short, but powerful devotionals encourage you to combine God's Word with prayer for a more intimate experience. The compilation of inspirational thoughts, scriptures, and prayers will help you discover God's wisdom for your life and what God holds true for your life.

978-1-934068-26-7

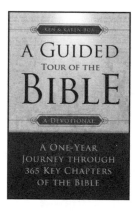

A GUIDED TOUR
OF THE BIBLE

A daily reading of 365 key chapters of the Bible provides the big picture of the principle people, events, and truths of scripture.

978-1-932805-92-5